OUR GOLDA
The Story of Golda Meir

ALSO BY DAVID A. ADLER

The Cam Jansen Adventure Series
Illustrated by Susanna Natti

*Hyperspace! Facts and Fun From
All Over the Universe*
Illustrated by Fred Winkowski

OUR GOLDA
The Story of Golda Meir

BY DAVID A. ADLER

Illustrated by Donna Ruff

THE VIKING PRESS
NEW YORK

Text Copyright © 1984 by David A. Adler
Illustrations Copyright © 1984 by Donna Ruff
All rights reserved
First published in 1984 by The Viking Press
40 West 23rd Street, New York, New York 10010
Published simultaneously in Canada by Penguin Books Canada Limited
Printed in U.S.A.
3   4   5   88   87   86   85

Library of Congress Cataloging in Publication Data
Adler, David A.   Our Golda, the story of Golda Meir.
Summary: A biography of the Israeli prime minister and world leader,
emphasizing her early childhood and youth in Russia and America.
1. Meir, Golda, 1898–1978—Juvenile literature.   2. Prime
ministers—Israel—Biography—Juvenile literature.
3. Zionists—Biography—Juvenile literature. [1. Meir, Golda,
1898–1978.   2. Prime ministers.   3. Israel—History]   I. Title.
DS126.6.M42A63   1984   956.94′053′0924   [B]   [92]   83-16798
ISBN 0-670-53107-3

To Mom, who, like Golda,
always thinks of others first

CONTENTS

Kiev   3

Pinsk   10

Milwaukee   16

Palestine   31

Israel   41

OUR GOLDA
The Story of Golda Meir

KIEV

Golda Meir was one of the great leaders of our time. She was the Prime Minister, the leader, of Israel. She was also a shopkeeper, schoolteacher, librarian, almond picker, and fund raiser. She was a chicken farmer, hunger striker, and freedom fighter. She was a mother and grandmother. She was Golda.

Golda moved rocks and planted trees. She carried guns past armed enemies. She argued with workers, soldiers, presidents, and kings.

Golda was tough, determined. She was strong.

Where did Golda get that strength?

Our Golda

She might have gotten it from her great-grandmother, Bobbe Golde. At the age of ninety-four Bobbe Golde still ruled her family. And she still poured salt in her tea to remind herself of the bitter taste of living outside the Jewish homeland. Young Golda was named after that great-grandmother. Some people even said Golda looked like her.

Golda's strength may have come from her grandfather. When he was only thirteen, he was kidnapped and forced to serve in the Russian army. The food Golda's grandfather was given in the army was not permitted by Jewish law. He wouldn't eat it. All during his many years in the army, he ate only bread and raw vegetables.

Golda's grandfather was ridiculed, threatened, and punished because he refused to become a Christian. When he was finally released, he was sure that somehow he had broken Jewish law. To punish himself, he slept for years, through cold Russian winters, on a flat wooden bench in an unheated synagogue.

Golda's parents were strong, too. They had to be. They were Jewish, and they lived in Russia under the rule of czars Alexander III and Nicholas II. It was in the late 1800s, a brutal, hungry, frightful time for Russian Jews.

Jews in Russia were not allowed to own land. Most were forced to live in a section called the "Pale of Settlement."

Jews were tailors, water carriers, fruit pickers, and woodcutters. Many worked twelve to twenty hours a day and earned only enough money to buy bread and water.

In 1881, not long before Golda was born, Jews were banished from Moscow, Tula, Riga, and other Russian cities. After that, the Moscow chief of police offered a reward to anyone in Moscow who caught a Jew. It was double the reward he offered for catching a thief.

And there were pogroms—planned riots against Jews. Russian police stood by and watched while mobs of workers and soldiers attacked the Jews. Doors were broken, windows shattered, and houses burned. Jews were robbed, beaten, and killed.

What did the Jews do to protect themselves? Mostly they hid. Many Russian Jews considered it wrong to fight, even when they were being attacked.

Once, when Golda's father heard a pogrom was coming, he boarded up the windows of the family's one-room apartment. Even four-year-old Golda knew that wood and nails wouldn't stop a mob of howling, laughing, shrieking men. Golda stood on the dark stairs of the building. She was frightened and angry that there was so little Jews could do to protect themselves. Luckily that day there was no pogrom.

Golda's father, Moshe Yitzhak Mabovitch, was tall, thin,

and strong. He was a carpenter and cabinetmaker and one of the first in his city to build a wooden icebox. Because of his skill, he was allowed to live outside the Pale of Settlement. But that didn't mean he could earn a living. He was often given work to do, but he was not always paid for it. One time, he was asked to build furniture for a government school. He hired extra workers. When the work was finished, the school kept the furniture, but because he was a Jew, Golda's father wasn't paid.

And what about Golda?

She was born May 3, 1898, in Kiev, Russia, a city outside the Pale. Times were hard then, even for a child. Six children were born into the family before Golda. Only one survived. The others died young, two when they were less than one year old. Golda might have died too if, before she was born, a wealthy family hadn't hired her mother to take care of their newborn baby. As part of the job, Golda's parents and her sister Sheyna moved from their small, damp room to a larger, brighter one.

Even with the better room, those were not easy days. There was not enough food for the family, not enough heat, and not enough warm clothes. Sheyna was nine years older than Golda. She often fainted in school from hunger. Then, when Golda was three, Tzipke, another girl, was born. Sometimes the watery porridge Golda was eating was taken off her plate to feed the baby.

Golda's father wandered far from home to find work. Some nights he came in from the cold and found there was not enough food to make him a meal. Days became weeks; weeks became months and years, and nothing changed. Then one night Golda's father said that he'd had enough. He would go to the *Goldene Medina*, the Golden Land—America. He sold most of what the family owned, including his woodworking

tools, and bought a boat ticket. He went off alone. Maybe he would earn enough to come back to "Mother Russia" a rich man. If not, he would surely earn enough to buy four more boat tickets so his family could join him in America.

That was 1903. Golda was five.

Golda and her family had been allowed to live outside the Pale of Settlement because her father was a skilled carpenter. When he left, Golda and her family were no longer allowed in Kiev. So they moved to Pinsk, a city within the Pale.

PINSK

*K*iev and Pinsk were very different. Kiev was a
large city with paved streets. Pinsk, a much smaller city, was
famous for its mud. The mud covered the streets and filled
the yards. There were also deep, muddy swamps, and Golda's
mother told her to keep away from them. But Golda didn't
always listen. One day she was playing with her friends near
a swampy area, and a pack of cruel Russian soldiers, Cossacks, suddenly appeared. They rode with their horses over
the terrified children. That convinced young Golda that the
swamps were dangerous. Cossacks lurked there, she believed,
just waiting to rise from the mud and attack the Jews.

10

To some people Pinsk wasn't a city of mud. It was a city of pigs. They were thin, hungry pigs, and they ran freely through the streets. Children chased after them. These wild pigs ran into people's homes, and before they ran out, they knocked over barrels of water and ate whatever scraps of food they found.

But mostly Pinsk was a city of workers. The people worked on the Pina and Pripet rivers. They fished, loaded and unloaded boats, and in the winter they hauled ice from the frozen rivers. The ice was buried in cellars and ditches, covered with straw, and saved for the summer. People in Pinsk worked in candle, plywood, match, and shoe-nail factories and flour mills.

Pinsk was a Jewish city. On the Sabbath and on Jewish holidays the factories were all closed.

What did the workers of Pinsk do when their factories were closed, when they weren't working? They went to synagogues and prayed. They visited friends, and they talked. And when they talked they drank tea. They argued and drank tea. There were people in Pinsk who could drink forty glasses of tea in a day. Some of them flavored their tea with strawberry or cherry jelly. Others held a sugar cube between their teeth and drank the tea through the sugar.

The people in Pinsk talked and argued about a Jewish

homeland. Many were Zionists, people who were working to establish a Jewish homeland in the land promised to the Jews in the Bible. It was Palestine then. Today it's Israel and Jordan. Others thought it would be easier and quicker to build the homeland in East Africa. And there were Bundists, people fighting for the rights of the workers.

Some of the talking and arguing took place in Golda's grandfather's tavern. That's where Golda and her family first lived when they moved to Pinsk. Golda's mother, Blume, worked in the kitchen. She helped serve the wine, beer, whiskey, and the meals. Golda and her two sisters didn't faint from hunger when they lived in Pinsk. When they lived above the tavern, there was always enough to eat.

The year Golda moved to Pinsk, 1903, there was a terrible pogrom in Kishinev, another Russian city within the Pale. The Kishinev chief of police encouraged the rioters. Five thousand of the Czar's soldiers stood by and did nothing to stop the violence. When the pogrom ended, forty-nine Jews were dead. More than five hundred Jews were badly hurt. Stores were robbed and burned. Thousands of Jewish families lost their homes.

In Paris, London, and New York, Jews gathered to protest the killings in Kishinev. Jews in Russia talked about fighting

back the next time and about working to overthrow the Czar. In Pinsk and elsewhere, Jews didn't eat or drink for an entire day in memory of the people who died in Kishinev.

When five-year-old Golda heard that the adults weren't eating, she refused to eat. Blume told her that it wasn't healthy for a young child to go without food. But Golda was tough, determined. She fasted the whole day in memory of the Jews who died in Kishinev.

Golda and her family didn't stay long in her grandfather's house. Blume baked and sold bread and cakes, and when she had enough money, she moved with her daughters into their own small apartment. Blume rented the apartment from an old butcher. It had two rooms. Set against the wall of one of the rooms was a large stone coal-burning oven. The top of the oven was flat and warm, a good place for someone as small as young Golda to rest. It was while Golda was up there that she heard her sister Sheyna talking with her friends about overthrowing the Czar. And they talked about building a Jewish homeland—a place where Jews could own land, where every school would be open to them, where there would be no pogroms.

Sheyna went to meetings in other homes, too. Sheyna, Golda, and their mother knew that if the police caught Sheyna at one of those meetings, she would be arrested and beaten. As punishment she might even be sent along with criminals and traitors to Siberia—a frozen, barren section of Russia. At night, while Blume and Golda waited for Sheyna to come home, they often heard screams coming from the nearby police station. Maybe those are Sheyna's screams, they thought. Maybe she was caught.

Then came the tragic year of 1905. Workers throughout Russia went on strike for shorter work days and for the freedom to speak and write as they pleased. Jewish workers in Pinsk joined the strike. A bomb exploded in Pinsk. Jews were arrested and beaten. A policeman was shot and killed. Jewish workers and Zionists were shot in the streets.

"Moshe, we can't stay here any longer," Blume wrote to her husband in America.

At first Moshe Mabovitch didn't have enough money to send for Blume and the girls. In New York, where Moshe lived when he first came to America, he was able to earn only three dollars a week. So he moved to Milwaukee, Wisconsin. There he got a job as a carpenter for a railroad, and in 1906 he sent for his family.

Blume, Sheyna, Golda, and Tzipke were going to America.

MILWAUKEE

*B*lume Mabovitch packed. She sewed coins, money for an emergency, into the hems of Sheyna's, Golda's, and Tzipke's dresses. They all said good-bye to their friends and family.

America was thousands of miles away. Blume and her daughters traveled by train and horse-drawn wagons from Russia, through Austria-Hungary and the German Empire to Belgium. On one train all their luggage disappeared. Blume had to take the coins hidden in her daughters' dresses to buy new clothes. Guards and drivers along the way asked for bribes. They lied to Blume to get the little money she had.

16

But Blume wasn't easily fooled. Then, when they reached Antwerp, a city of Belgium along the shore of the North Sea, Blume, Sheyna, Golda, and Tzipke boarded a ship bound for America.

They spent two weeks on that ship. It was crowded with hundreds of other poor, pale, and frightened people who had left Russia. At night they slept in a dark, cramped cabin deep down in the ship's hold. Blume, Sheyna, and Tzipke were sick most of the time. But Golda wasn't. She stood on deck and looked across the ocean.

Our Golda

The ordeal wasn't over when the ship docked in New York. Inspectors were waiting for them, yelling at Blume and her daughters to hurry and get in line. The children were asked a question, any question, just to check if they could hear, if they could talk. Doctors poked in their hair, their ears, their eyes. They were looking for disease. Anyone who wasn't healthy would be sent back to Russia.

Blume, Sheyna, Golda, and Tzipke were allowed into America, but they were still not near their new home. They traveled by train for nine hundred more miles to Milwaukee, Wisconsin.

Milwaukee in 1906 was a big city, much bigger than Pinsk, even bigger than Kiev. It was a city with beautiful parks and squares, with three rivers, and near the great Lake Michigan. Steamboats traveled across the lake, carrying coal and grain. Railroads connected Milwaukee with the rest of the country.

The parents in almost every Milwaukee family had been born outside the United States. Most of them came from Germany. They traded coal, lumber, grain, and flour. They worked in factories, making men's clothing, shoes, furniture, and machines. And they made beer. More beer was made in Milwaukee than anywhere else in the country.

When Blume, Sheyna, Golda, and Tzipke came to Milwaukee, Moshe met them at the railroad station. He was a changed man. His clothes were different—American-looking. His beard was gone. To his daughter Golda, he seemed a stranger.

That night Moshe took his family to his small rented room. The next morning he took them shopping. Golda was fascinated by the cars, trolleys, and bicycles, the barber shop chairs and the cigar store Indians. She watched the constant stream of people who crowded the sidewalks and stores. She stared at women wearing long white skirts, men wearing colored neckties, and at a little girl pushing a toy baby carriage with a doll inside.

Milwaukee was an exciting place for Golda. When they arrived, she rode from the railroad station in a car. It was the first car Golda had ever been in. The next day Golda was in Shuster's Department Store. It had five floors and was the tallest building young Golda had ever seen. To her it was a skyscraper.

Golda loved the soda pop, ice cream, and new American clothes her father bought for her and her sisters. But Sheyna didn't. Her father was struggling to be a "real American," but Sheyna refused to change. She was determined to keep fighting for the rights of workers and for a Jewish homeland. And she would continue wearing her black dress with its

high collar and long sleeves, just as she had in Pinsk.

Golda's mother was determined, too. Her family wouldn't be poor. And they wouldn't all live crowded together in one small room. She quickly found them a new apartment. This one had two rooms, a kitchen, and a long narrow hall that led to an empty shop. Soon after they moved in, Blume filled the shop with milk, cheese, butter, and bread and opened a dairy store.

Golda hated that store. Every morning her mother went to the market to buy fresh milk and eggs. While Golda's friends were on their way to school, Golda had to watch the store, measure out cups of flour and sugar for the customers, cut cheese, and wrap loaves of bread. She often came late to class.

One day a police officer came to the house to talk about Golda's lateness. Golda's mother listened and smiled as he told her that in America children had to go to school, that they had to be on time. But the officer was talking in English, and like most Jews who came to America, Blume spoke only Yiddish. She hardly understood a word the officer said.

Golda continued to work in the store and come late to school. But she was a good student. She learned English quickly, and in the fourth grade she became involved in her first community project. She organized the American Young

Sisters Society. It was a name she made up. She was only eleven years old, but she rented a room for a meeting. She sent out invitations and spoke to the crowd of adults who came.

Blume begged Golda to write out her speech. But Golda refused. She preferred just to stand up and talk, to tell the people what was on her mind and in her heart. Over the years Golda made thousands of speeches. She almost always spoke the same way, from her heart, without notes.

Golda told the people who came to the meeting that there were children in Milwaukee who were too poor to buy schoolbooks. After Golda spoke, Tzipke read a Yiddish poem.

Money was collected. Books were bought. And for the first time, a newspaper printed an article all about Golda.

While Golda was in school, her older sister, Sheyna, was working in a cluttered, dusty factory sewing buttonholes. Sheyna was a small, frail woman, and she worked long, hard hours. She was often tired, and many times the needle pierced one of her fingers instead of the cloth. Then Sheyna got sick. She had tuberculosis, a common illness among factory workers. She was sent hundreds of miles away to a hospital in Denver, Colorado. It was one of the best hospitals for people with her illness.

· *Milwaukee* ·

When Sheyna recovered, she stayed in Denver and married Shamai Korngold, her sweetheart from Pinsk. After Sheyna had left for America, Shamai had been arrested for talking against the Czar. He escaped from jail, came to America, and followed Sheyna, first to Milwaukee and then to Denver.

Blume was furious when she heard about her daughter's marriage. To her, Shamai was a lunatic with grand ideas and empty pockets. What kind of life could he give Sheyna?

Golda wrote to Sheyna about school and about the summer job that she and her friend Regina had, wrapping packages in a department store. Golda earned eight and a half cents an hour on that job. She used the money she earned to buy a winter coat. Golda also wrote to Sheyna about the arguments she had with her parents.

Many of the arguments were about Mr. Goodstein. He was a successful man. He bought, sold, and rented rooms and apartments. Mr. Goodstein had met Golda in her mother's store. He talked to Golda, liked her, and wanted to marry her. Golda's parents wanted the marriage. But Mr. Goodstein was in his thirties and Golda was only fourteen. She refused to marry him.

Golda wanted to stay in school and become a teacher. But teachers in Milwaukee were not allowed to be married. When Golda's parents heard that, they wanted her out of school.

Our Golda

She had learned enough, they said. It was time for her to get a job and a husband.

Golda's sister Sheyna and her husband didn't agree. "You shouldn't stop school," Shamai wrote to Golda. "You have a good chance to become something. My advice is that you should get ready and come to us."

Golda wanted to go to Denver, to Sheyna and Shamai, and finish school there. But Golda knew that her parents wouldn't let her leave Milwaukee. She decided to run away.

Sheyna and Shamai sent money for Golda's railway ticket, but it wasn't enough. So Golda and her good friend Regina gave English lessons to "greeners"—people who had just arrived in America. The pay was ten cents an hour.

When they had all the money they needed, Regina worked out a plan for Golda's escape. One night Golda tied her clothes in a bundle and dropped them from her second-floor window. Regina ran with the bundle to the railway station, checked it in the baggage room, and went home.

Golda wrote a note to her parents, explaining that she was going to Sheyna's to study. There was nothing to worry about; she would write to them from Denver. Golda kissed her sleeping sister Tzipke good-bye and waited for morning.

The next morning, when Golda's parents saw her leave the house with her books, they thought she was on her way to

school. But she was on her way to the railway station. Golda
never thought to look at the train schedule. She sat in the
Milwaukee railway station waiting for a train to Denver. She
was still sitting there when her parents found her note. But
they also never thought to look at a train schedule. They
thought she was already on her way. It wasn't until late that
afternoon that Golda boarded a train for Denver.

Sheyna's apartment was a gathering place for young Jewish
thinkers. When Golda wasn't in school, studying, or press-
ing pants in Shamai's dry-cleaning store, she was serving tea
in Sheyna's apartment. And she was listening. She heard talk
in that apartment about a world without czars, kings, or
presidents, a world without governments. She heard that the
world wasn't fair to workers, women, or Jews. And she heard
that happiness was not important; fighting for the rights of
others was.

In Sheyna's apartment Golda also met Morris Meyerson.
While others argued, he listened. When he did speak, he
spoke softly. He was a gentle, quiet man, a sign painter who
loved music and poetry. He gave fifteen-year-old Golda lists
of books to read and he took her to free concerts in the
park.

Then, two years after Golda left Milwaukee, a letter came

from her father. It was the only letter he wrote to her in Denver. He asked Golda to please come home. She could finish school in Milwaukee.

Golda knew that it must have been difficult for her father to write that letter. I must really be wanted, needed, at home, Golda thought. She prepared to go back to Milwaukee.

Morris couldn't go with Golda. But before she left, he quietly told Golda that he loved her. He wanted to marry her. And Golda told Morris that she loved him, too.

Golda's parents had moved from the apartment behind the store. Their new apartment was a busy place. When Golda's mother, Blume, cooked and baked, there was often a friend or neighbor keeping her company, telling Blume her troubles and asking for help. When a Yiddish writer came to Milwaukee, or when someone came to Milwaukee to speak about the need for a Jewish homeland, Golda's father often invited him to sleep on their living-room couch. When World War I started and young men from Milwaukee joined the fighting Jewish Legion to free Palestine from the Turks, Blume fed the soldiers. She sewed for them and sent them off with bags filled with warm cakes and cookies.

During World War I, as armies marched through Europe and parts of Russia, Jews were forced from their homes. In

Our Golda

Pinsk, where Golda once lived, Jews were lined up and shot. Golda stood on a box at street corners and spoke against the violence.

Golda's father heard about her speeches. He agreed with what Golda was saying, but he didn't want his daughter standing on street corners. He told Golda that if she went back to the street to speak, he would grab her by the hair and pull her home. But that night Golda was at the corner again, telling people what was happening to innocent Jews. Golda's father came to take her home. But he stood and listened. She spoke so well that he forgot all about his threat to drag her home.

Golda also organized a march through the streets of Milwaukee to let people know what was happening to Jews. But even as Golda marched, she knew that speeches and parades were not enough. Jews needed their own land.

Morris wrote to Golda. He came to visit her. They went to concerts. They talked about many things, but they didn't always agree. Morris didn't believe that a homeland would help the Jews. But they did love each other, and in December 1917 she and Morris Meyerson were married.

Golda and Morris were married just one month after Arthur James Balfour, an important British official, declared in a letter that his government believed the Jews should have a

homeland in Palestine. That letter became known as the Balfour Declaration. And to Golda, who was already planning to move with Morris to Palestine, that declaration meant that her dream of a Jewish homeland might one day come true.

PALESTINE

When they were first married, Morris worked as a sign painter and Golda had a job for Poalei Zion, a group working to establish a Jewish homeland in Palestine. Golda traveled by train to cities across the United States and Canada to speak for Poalei Zion at meetings and conventions.

Golda was paid fifteen dollars a week for her work, and when she traveled, Poalei Zion paid her expenses. But Golda's travel expenses never included hotel bills. She saved the Poalei Zion money by staying with friends. Golda also didn't ask them to pay for the desserts she ate after dinner. "Poalei

Zion doesn't owe me ice cream," Golda said. She paid for that herself.

While Golda was away, Morris went to the theater and to concerts. And he decorated the walls of their tiny apartment with pictures cut from magazines. When Golda came home, Morris was always waiting for her with a handful of freshly cut flowers.

Golda and Morris saved their money, and in the spring of 1921 they felt ready to leave for Palestine. They sold their chairs, tables, beds, curtains, and winter clothes. Morris wouldn't sell his records or his wind-up record player, though. He was willing to be a pioneer, but he wouldn't give up his music.

Golda and Morris traveled with Sheyna, her family, and some friends for almost two months. Most of the journey was spent on a dreadful little ship, the S.S. *Pocahontas*. During their voyage there was a fire on board, the engines broke down several times, the sailors protested the poor conditions on the ship by throwing salt on the passenger's food, mixing salty seawater with the drinking water, and smashing the ship's refrigerator. One of the sailors went mad and had to be locked in chains.

The *Pocahontas* took Golda, Morris, and the others to Italy, where they boarded another ship to Egypt. From there they took a train to Tel Aviv, a Jewish city in Palestine. From the train Golda looked out of her window and saw her homeland for the first time. She saw sand, a huge unending sea of it. When the group finally got off that train, they felt the full force of Tel Aviv's hot summer sun. One of the men in Golda's group said that he'd seen enough of his homeland. He was ready to leave.

During the next few days the group found bedbugs in their rooms. They went to a Tel Aviv marketplace and found it thick with flies. They met Jews, refugees from an Arab riot, living in tents pitched in the sand. The neighboring Arab city of Jaffa was worse. Its streets were crowded with mad, blind, and crippled beggars, lepers, people clothed in rags. But Golda and Morris stayed. And so did the man who said that he'd seen enough.

During those early years of the new Jewish community in Palestine, Jews all over the world, even very poor Jews, were dropping coins into blue tin collection boxes. Those coins added up to the large sums of money needed to buy land from the Arabs. At about the time Golda and Morris came to Palestine, a large tract of barren swampland was bought for a Jewish settlement. That's where Golda decided to work.

Golda and Morris tried to join Merhavyah. It was a kibbutz, a small community of people who worked together and shared everything they earned and owned. At first the thirty men and seven women of Merhavyah didn't want Golda. They were sure that she was a "spoiled American girl" who couldn't spend long days working in the hot sun. Later, when Golda and Morris were accepted, Golda felt sure the group welcomed them only so they could listen to the records Morris brought from America.

Golda and Morris worked hard planting trees, picking almonds, feeding and milking the cows, paving roads, and building houses. Golda ran the Merhavyah chicken coops. And in the kitchen Golda often cooked hot oatmeal and chickpea mush, and made coffee for everyone in the kibbutz.

Golda and Morris stayed at Merhavyah for more than two years. But Morris wasn't happy there. Golda was often too busy to be with him. There were a great many rules he didn't like, and he missed the chance to read and go to concerts. Morris was often sick. A few times he had the chills and high fever of malaria, a disease carried through the swamps by infected mosquitoes. The doctor told Golda that the hot sun, hard work, and poor food were too much for Morris.

Golda and Morris left Merhavyah and moved to a small two-room apartment in Jerusalem. They had no gas or electricity. All their heat and light came from an oil-burning stove. Morris had a job as a bookkeeper, but he was paid very little for his work. It was a real struggle to buy food and oil for the stove, and to pay the rent.

While Golda and Morris lived in Jerusalem, their two children, Menachem and Sarah, were born. Golda loved them, but she missed Merhavyah, the people there and the work.

After four years at home with the children, Golda went to work as a secretary for the Histadrut, the Jewish labor union in Palestine. She quickly became one of its leaders. But Golda was away so often that Morris wasn't happy. During Golda's years at the Histadrut, Morris moved out, came back, and moved out again. They never divorced, but during much of their marriage Golda and Morris lived apart.

Golda was always busy working, making speeches and running to meetings. Sometimes, when Golda traveled, she took the children with her. But often they stayed with Golda's sister Sheyna.

In the 1930s Golda and the other leaders of the Histadrut and Jews throughout the world faced difficult problems. The Arabs in Palestine were overturning buses and trains. They attacked and killed Jews. Golda called for Jews to defend themselves but not to seek revenge.

At the same time, in Germany, the Nazis took away the rights of Jews to work, go to school, and own property. They attacked and destroyed Jewish stores and synagogues. And as the Nazis became more powerful, they forced Jews into work camps, concentration camps—death camps. They tortured Jews. They gassed and killed Jewish men, women, and children.

Golda went to France, to a meeting on the "Jewish Problem." Leaders from more than twenty countries spoke. But no one was willing to open the doors of his country to the homeless, persecuted Jews. Then Golda spoke. "These are human beings, not numbers," she said. "Let them come to Palestine. We're poor, but we'll gladly share the crumbs of our poverty with them." But the British ruled Palestine, and soon after the meeting they announced that for the next five years only a limited number of Jews would be allowed into Palestine. After that, none at all.

During the Nazi period boatloads of Jews running for safety came to Palestine. The British sent them back. In Europe Jews hid in barns, forests, cellars, attics, sewers, and graveyards. There were rallies and protests. But in the end six million men, women, and children were murdered—because they were Jews.

After the war two boatloads of Jews, one thousand survivors, were stopped on their way to Palestine. The British still wouldn't let them in. But the Jews wouldn't get off the ships.

Our Golda

They refused to eat. They would rather starve than go back. In Palestine Golda and a group she organized stopped eating, too. Then after more than one hundred hours without food, the British let the boats sail. But most boatloads of Jews were not let into Palestine. Many thousands of Jews, people who lived through the German Nazi terror, were forced by the British to return to Germany.

In 1947 Golda went to a camp in Cyprus—a camp of huts and tents, guarded by watchtowers and barbed-wire fences. It was a British camp for Jews who had survived the Nazis. Every month the British were allowing seven hundred and fifty Jews to leave the camp in Cyprus for Palestine. Golda arranged for the children to be the first to go. While Golda was in the camp, two young children gave her a bouquet of paper flowers. Those flowers were from children too young to remember ever living outside wire fences. They were from children who perhaps had never seen a real flower growing in a field. Those flowers were a gift that Golda never forgot.

The years after the war, 1946 and 1947, were bloody years in Palestine. Arabs hid in the hills and attacked Jews traveling on the roads below. The British arrested and hanged Jewish freedom fighters. Jews blew up railroads, bridges, boats, and British army headquarters.

The problems in Palestine were brought before the United

Nations, and in November 1947 the member nations voted on a partition plan. It would cut Palestine into an Arab state and a Jewish state. The Jewish state would be small. It wouldn't include Jerusalem. But it would be a state, a Jewish state.

Jews throughout Palestine sat with pencil and paper near radios and recorded the vote. Afghanistan: no. Argentina: abstained; they refused to take sides. Australia: yes. Belgium: yes. Brazil: yes. Cuba: no. In the end thirty-three nations voted yes, including the United States and Russia. Thirteen nations voted no. Ten, including the British, abstained. The resolution passed. Within a few months the British would leave Palestine and the Jews would have a homeland.

Jews crowded the streets of Palestine to celebrate. But Golda knew there would be trouble. She stood on the balcony of her office and spoke to the crowd, but she was really speaking to the many Arabs in Palestine. "Let us now live in friendship and peace togther," she said.

At the United Nations the Arabs were bitter. The vote would lead to war, they said. Then they walked out.

The next day there was violence. While British police stood by and watched, Arabs burned Jewish stores in Jerusalem and killed five Jews who were riding in a bus. If the Jews wanted a homeland, they would have to fight for it.

ISRAEL

War. It began even before the British left Palestine. The Arabs in Palestine didn't want a Jewish state, no matter how small.

Palestine became a land of barbed wire, blackened windows, watchmen, guns, and homemade bombs. Water pipes were blown up. Cars, trucks, and buildings exploded.

The Arab nations surrounding Palestine had guns, tanks, and bombs. The British sold arms to the Arabs. They trained and helped support soldiers in the Arab Legion. But the British wouldn't allow the Jews to own weapons. Jewish soldiers trained in secret, using sticks for rifles. The Jews knew that

41

when the British left, the armies of the nearby Arab states would attack. The Jews needed to buy more guns. And for that they needed money.

At a meeting in Tel Aviv it was decided that Golda would go to America to raise money. She left that meeting and went straight to the airport. She arrived in New York in the middle of a winter blizzard, carrying just her handbag. She hadn't even brought along a coat.

Golda spoke first to a conference in Chicago, Illinois. As usual, she spoke without notes. She spoke from her heart.

Golda told her audience about a group of students who had been on their way to help defend a Jewish settlement. They were attacked by Arabs. Later, when their bodies were found, some of the students still held stones in their hands. "If we have guns to fight with," Golda told the people in

Chicago, "we will fight with them. If not, we will fight with stones in our hands.

"The spirit is there. This spirit alone cannot face rifles and machine guns. . . . You cannot decide whether we should fight or not. We will. . . . You can only decide one thing. Whether we shall be victorious."

The audience stood up. They cheered. Golda raised many millions of dollars in America, more than she had dreamed possible. When Golda came home, David Ben-Gurion, the leader of the Jews in Palestine, said, "Someday, when history will be written, it will be said that there was a Jewish woman who got the money which made the State possible."

Then, two months later, just a few days before the British

were to leave Palestine, Golda went on a secret mission. She put on black Arab robes and a veil. She traveled late at night and changed cars twice so she wouldn't be followed. Golda didn't want the Arabs to know she was going to see King Abdullah, the Arab king of Jordan. Several months before, he had promised not to join the war against the Jews. Golda asked him to keep his promise. The Jews wanted peace. But the king said he couldn't stay out of an Arab war. As soon as Israel was declared a state, his army would join the armies of Egypt, Syria, Lebanon, and Iraq and fight to destroy Israel.

During the next few months in Israel there were shootings, roadblocks, attacks, and bombings. The Arabs were fighting to keep Israel from being born, and the Jews were fighting back. When Arab citizens heard that Jewish fighters were coming, they ran from their homes. In one city, Haifa, as Arabs ran to boats and British trucks to leave the city, Golda called to them through loudspeakers to persuade them to stay and be part of the Jewish state. They could be citizens of Israel with the same rights as the Jews. But they wouldn't stay.

In the United Nations there were speeches, meetings, and arranged cease-fires. When the fighting ended, there was a Jewish state. Israel still controlled the land the United Nations had set aside for it. But there was no Arab state of Palestine. In the fighting Israel had captured some of the land. All the rest was taken by the Arab states of Jordan and Egypt.

On May 14, 1948, Israel was declared a state. When Golda signed the Declaration of Independence, her eyes filled with tears. They were tears of happiness. And they were tears for the millions of Jews who hadn't lived to see the new state, Jews who hadn't lived because there was no Jewish state.

Our Golda

Soon after Israel became a state, Golda was sent to Moscow. She was Israel's first ambassador to Russia. While she was there, she went to teas and dinners. She met with diplomats and newsmen. And she met Jews, the "silent Jews" of Russia. They were not allowed to study Hebrew, celebrate Jewish holidays, or even bake matzah for Passover. Their rabbis were often arrested and jailed. The Russian government was against religion, and anyone who openly spoke about his Jewishness put himself in danger.

On Rosh Ha-Shanah, the Jewish New Year, Golda went to the Moscow synagogue. Thousands of Jews greeted her. And when she left, they crowded around Golda, stretched out to touch her, to kiss her dress. *"Nasha Golda*—our Golda," they said. To them, Golda was a part of Israel. It was their homeland, too.

Golda knew how difficult it was for them to come to greet

her. "Thank you," Golda told them, "for remaining Jews."

A few days later Golda was in the Moscow synagogue again. It was Yom Kippur, the holiest day of the Jewish year. At the end of the service, when Jews traditionally pray that next year they would be in Jerusalem, the entire congregation looked up at Golda. She knew then that it was important to Jews throughout the world that Israel survive.

While Golda was in Russia, Israel had its first elections. David Ben-Gurion became Prime Minister, the leader of the

new nation. He asked Golda to be Israel's first Minister of Labor.

When Golda returned to Israel, Jews were already pouring into the country. They came from Turkey, Poland, Rumania, and Yemen. Jewish refugees came from Arab countries. Jews who had lost their homes and families during the Nazi period came from Germany, Austria, Italy, and Cyprus. Thousands of Jews came each week. They all needed food, clothing, and health care. Their children needed schools.

The Jews who came were mostly poor, and it was hard for Israel to take care of them all. Many people felt that Israel should slow the flood of people. But Golda said that she and others had fought for a homeland, and a home must keep its doors open. Jews, no matter how many, no matter how poor, must always be welcome in Israel.

Golda visited the new citizens of Israel in their tents and metal huts. As Minister of Labor she insisted that houses be built for them. Houses were also built for the Arabs who were still in Israel but who had lost their homes during the War of Independence. Golda changed the building plans so that each tiny new house had an indoor toilet and a window over the kitchen sink so, while the women worked, they could look outside and watch their children. Golda helped set up schools to teach the new citizens to become plumbers, electricians, and farmers. She worked to create jobs, build roads, and set up funds for widows and orphans. Golda was happiest when she was helping people. She often said that the seven years she spent as Minister of Labor were the happiest years of her life.

In 1956 Ben-Gurion asked Golda to become Foreign Minister. He also asked her to change her name. Ben-Gurion felt that German, Russian, and English last names were ties to other countries. He had changed his name from Gruen. Other Israelis had changed their names, too. And Golda changed her name from Meyerson to Meir, which means "to give light."

While Golda was Foreign Minister, Israel sent money and people to help poor African nations. Golda visited Africa, and once, while she was there, she was on a bus with some black African leaders. They were on their way to see Victoria Falls, the world's highest waterfall. Their bus was stopped, and the blacks were told to separate from the whites. Golda refused to go on. If she couldn't be with her friends, she didn't want to see the falls at all. The bus turned around and went back.

In 1965, after nine years as Foreign Minister, Golda retired. But not completely. She still worked for her political party, the Mapai. She also still held a seat in the Knesset, a branch of the Israeli government like the Congress of the United States.

During those few somewhat quiet years Golda shopped, cooked, washed, ironed, and did housework. She visited her grown children and grandchildren.

But those weren't quiet years for Israel. In 1967 Egypt blocked all ships from reaching Israel's port of Eilat. Thousands of tanks and armed Arab soldiers stood on Israel's borders in Egypt, Syria, and Jordan, ready to attack. Early in June Prime Minister Levi Eshkol led Israel in a war against those three neighboring countries. Six days later, when the fighting stopped, Israel had a remarkable victory and held huge areas of Arab land.

Then in February 1969 Levi Eshkol, Golda's good friend and Israel's leader, died. Golda was selected as Israel's new Prime Minister. The Arabs called her "Golda Lox" and "Old Lady." Newspaper reporters called her "Israel's Uncrowned Queen." At first she was chosen by Israel's leaders to be Prime Minister only until there could be new elections. But in October the people voted, and seventy-one-year-old Golda was chosen to continue as their leader.

In Israel during Golda's five years as Prime Minister, a great number of houses and factories were built. Israel also built its first jet, the Commodore. And thousands of Jews were allowed to leave Russia and settle in Israel. But there was also trouble. Arab terrorists bombed a school bus, the Tel Aviv bus station, the Hebrew University, and a Jerusalem food market. Planes to Israel were hijacked. Israeli athletes at the Olympic games in Munich, Germany, were murdered.

In her search for peace Golda met secretly in Paris with King Hussein of Jordan, and she met with Pope Paul VI. But she was also preparing for war. Soon after she became Prime Minister, she went to Washington to meet President Nixon. She gave him a list of the weapons Israel would need for defense against an Arab attack.

That attack came in October 1973 on Yom Kippur, the holiest day of the Jewish year. Huge forces of Egyptian and Syrian soldiers, tanks and bombers surprised Israel. Thousands of Israeli soldiers, many coming straight from synagogues, rushed to join the fighting. A few days later Iraq and then Jordan joined in the war against Israel. But after more than two weeks of heavy fighting, when a cease-fire was declared, Israel's forces were in control. They had moved into Syria and crossed the Suez Canal into Egypt.

After the war there was an outcry in Israel against Golda and her government. Thousands of soldiers had died in the fighting. Why hadn't Israel been ready? But the people of

51

Our Golda

Israel still wanted Golda to lead them, and in the elections soon after the war, Golda was again made Prime Minister.

Golda stayed on for only a few more months. Then, in 1974, at the age of seventy-six, Golda resigned.

During the next few years Golda met with important world leaders and spoke before large groups of people. In one speech before an American audience Golda explained why she first went to Palestine in 1921.

"I was selfish," she said. "I heard something was going on over there, something was being built, and I said, 'What? And I won't have a share in it? No. I'm going.' "

Golda also wrote *My Life*, a book that told her life story, from Kiev and Pinsk to the State of Israel. In it she wrote that she had a dream that was still with her. It was a dream of Arabs crossing the border with tractors and not tanks, with their hands stretched out in friendship. In 1977, shortly before Golda died, she met Anwar Sadat, the President of Egypt, who had come to Israel seeking peace. It seemed that her dream of *shalom*, peace, might someday come true.

ABOUT THE BOOK

DAVID A. ADLER is the author of all the titles in the Cam Jansen Adventure Series, *Hyperspace! Facts and Fun From All Over the Universe* (all Viking), and several books about Jewish history and culture. He lives with his wife and son in Woodmere, New York.

Mr. Adler carefully researched the cities where Golda lived by reading biographies of Golda's contemporaries, as well as encyclopedias and newspapers of that period. "When I was still a child," he says, "Mrs. Meir was already the Foreign Minister of Israel. But in my home we referred to her affectionately as 'Golda,' as if she were a close personal friend."

DONNA RUFF taught art and art history in Florida before becoming a freelance illustrator. She now lives in New York City with her son.

For the jacket painting, Ms. Ruff combined colored inks, pencils, and pastels. The inside illustrations were done with soft pencil.